# Finally...Monologues that Work (Ages 4-18)

*Laurie Ann Davis and Christine Kolenik*

*Foreword By Glenn Alterman*

Bloomington, IN  Milton Keynes, UK

authorHOUSE®

*AuthorHouse™*
*1663 Liberty Drive, Suite 200*
*Bloomington, IN 47403*
*www.authorhouse.com*
*Phone: 1-800-839-8640*

*AuthorHouse™ UK Ltd.*
*500 Avebury Boulevard*
*Central Milton Keynes, MK9 2BE*
*www.authorhouse.co.uk*
*Phone: 08001974150*

*First published by AuthorHouse 9/28/2006*

*ISBN: 1-4259-5987-3 (sc)*

*Printed in the United States of America*
*Bloomington, Indiana*

*This book is printed on acid-free paper.*

# FOREWORD

I think what fascinated me most about Laurie Davis and Christine Kolenik's book was their ability to capture in monologue form, a child's voice and thinking. As I read the monologues I felt like I was actually listening to a child speak. I've written many books of original monologues, but when it came to writing children's monologues, I always found the task somewhat daunting. I guess I just didn't have the ability to think as a child does, as these authors do.

What I also admired about this book was that many of the monologues dealt with issues that children face every day; the small squabbles, sibling stuff, friendship issues, etc. But there are also other pieces that resonate more deeply. There's material here about winning and losing in life, relationships, and how to cope with the world as you're growing up. Loss, love, and first attractions are all handled in a sensitive and caring way. Aside from being just good audition material, there are life lessons here.

Being a child actor is difficult enough. Finding a good monologue for an audition shouldn't have to be. Yet there are very few good children's monologue books on the market today. Some of the students that I coach at The Glenn Alterman Studio in New York City, are children as young as eleven years old. To give the material a fair test, I asked several of my students to read the monologues aloud. Not only did the material read beautifully, but the children seemed to genuinely enjoy them. Some of their comments were, "My sisters just like this girl", or "That sounds just like me and my brother, I swear", or "I know exactly what she's talking about!"

The monologues are just the right length for agent and theater auditions. They vary as to subject matter, content, and type. Bottom line, there's something here for every child actor, no matter what their training has been.

You can tell that this book was written with care, concern, and love. Even in their introduction, the authors express their sincere desire to help children succeed in a business that's very tough. I feel that they've made a worth while contribution. Believe me, you won't find a better monologue book for your child than this one. Best of luck.

Glenn Alterman
The Glenn Alterman Studio
New York, NY

# Dedications

I would like to dedicate this book to my baby boy Saverio Pelice Potente (Dozzy). To my beautiful boy Saverio thank you for your love and inspiration. You make me smile, laugh and create. You are my light, my strength. I love you so very much. -Mommy Special thanks to my sister Barbara and my brother-in-law Tommy for believing in me and supporting me. To my Uncle Bernie Davis for all his help and support. To my beautiful friend Christine who's never ending friendship and talent made this book possible. To Karen Farley for your friendship and help, and to all my students past and present you are the inspiration for my writing and my teaching. To Dawn and Brittany for all your support and faith in me. To my mom and dad for giving me life. Mom, I hope this gets you up and running. To my brother Michael and his wife Mary for their love. To Patrick and Delores Kolenik for all your support and for creating Christine. And to my voice teacher David Russell who said to me "You must teach." David, you were and always will be my favorite teacher; a guide and a force who pushed me to a place I thought I never could have gone. I wish I was able to tell you that and to say goodbye. To all the actors and artists and musicians who have inspired me throughout my life; especially Joanne Woodward and Paul Newman (the two actor's whose work inspired me to become a creative force). Long live the King and Queen. And my special student Theresa Bivona. You left us too soon. I see you in my dreams on the stage acting, dancing and singing and being the star you were meant to be. Thank you for thinking I was something special. And to Glenn Alterman who said "You should write." I did as soon as I hung up the phone and haven't stopped since. To Jim Bonney for an acting foundation that can withstand a tornado. To Chris Cardona for all your help with the my web-site. A special dedication to my niece's Nicole and Emily and nephew Zachary and Rob. And to God for giving me a second chance. I hope I won't disappoint you!  I would also like to thank myself for having the courage to plant the seeds and for giving myself the time to water my own garden and now I look forward to watching it grow.

-Laurie Ann Davis

I would not have been able to write any of this and follow my dreams if it wasn't for my family and friends. You have all inspired me in so many incredible ways. Thank you Mom and Dad for being the most amazing parents and believing in my dreams. Thank you Lauren for being the best sister ever and constantly challenging me. Thank you grandma for being a constant source of love. Thank you Matt for your support, care and insight. I love you all more then you could ever imagine! Thank you Laurie for being a wonderful friend and a talented person; you started this process and have taught me and many people a lot. Thank you to all of my Cold Spring Harbor friends. You have all helped shape who I am as a person, and I have gotten a lot of material from our experiences together. I love you all so much! To my amazing friend Missy; thanks for fantasizing with me about the future and dreaming some big dreams. Thank you Kat for being my friend since, well since forever. To Tricia, Chris and Jeanine; thank you for sharing your creative gifts with me and for being such a special part of my life. Thank you to Scott Alan. You are amazingly talented and I have learned so much from you! Thank you Shannon and Doug for always being there. Thank you to the cast of "Friends." Whenever I want to give up, I watch your show and what you do and it reminds me of what a magical profession this is. You guys are amazing. Most of all I would like to thank my grandfather Vito Zichitella, to whom I dedicate this book. Through you I have learned kindness, hard work the true meaning of family. I miss and love you so much!

-Christine Kolenik

# Thank You

We would like to thank author Glenn Alterman who's many books and monologues have inspired us to write. Having performed his works many times as actors and using his material with our students, we have found no one better. It goes without saying that auditioning with Glenn's monologues always work.

Thank you Glenn for a wonderful forward, your encouragement and time. We look forward to your next book and the one after that and the one after that............

Glenn Alterman Studios<br>
New York, NY

We would also like to thank Daureen Castonguay of Wilhelmina Models Inc. and Michael Guy of Atlas Talent Agency, Inc. for their kind words and taking the time to read and support our book.

# Table of Contents

# Introduction

Don't ever settle. Even when its something that can be small enough as picking a monologue. As actors, we spend countless hours, days, weeks, months, years delving, digging trying to scrap up the one that fits us; the one that makes us feel something; the one that clicks. When picking a monologue, it's important to believe in what you're saying...in what you do. For an actor, having the perfect monologue in your back pocket is crucial. You have to believe in the words, the meaning. You need to relate. Believe us, we know how hard it is to find that perfect monologue. The one that you can't do without. The one that jumps out at you like an uncontrollable force. At one time we thought this might be one of our biggest challenges as actors, until we became "acting teachers." Then the real challenge began. We were to start off on yet another search, only this time we were looking for the perfect monologue for children ranging from the ages of 4-18. Hard work it was, but we persisted, book after book, going through each one with a student in mind. Could we find one that would work for them, one they would like, one that would bring out the best in them? No, it didn't happen. Our hard work went unnoticed. As we handed out monologue after monologue we heard cries of "I don't like this one", "I don't feel it" or just plain "I would never say this."

We begged, we pleaded and well we came up empty handed. Until one day the acting light bulb came on. A 10 year old girl walked into the studio and told a story of how she was being picked on in school and how she now hated going and was scared. She wanted a monologue that could help her deal with her emotions, to help her let things out. Something she could use in her acting. We thought, hmm..what if we write something for you? Oh, but can we write? Well, we found out that we could write and write and write. The more the children talked, the more we wrote. The complaining turned into cheers of "This is funny," "This made me feel so many things." "This one's me!," and our favorite "This one is fun to do." We hope that you can find a monologue in this book that does this for you, your child or client. If you can't, then please buy another book and search again.

This book was meant as a glossary to the soul of a child. The monologues deal with real issues and real things that we all go through in a way that does not patronize. You may find some of the pieces to be very raw and bold, but that's life. You can't sugar coat the true deep emotions of a child learning to grow and becoming ones self. If you find some of the monologues not relatable to you because you are only looking at the ones in your age range, then don't do that one. Pick another one. If you are only twelve, but think you can handle a monologue that we arbitrarily dubbed to be for a teenager then do it. If it speaks to you, sings to you, by all means dive into it. The ages were merely meant as guidelines. Most of the times we really just used it as an organizational tool for ourselves, so there was some sort of structure to the book. Do what you like. You're an actor and a kid. You have everyone around you telling you what to do and what rules to follow. Well, we are giving you no rules. We say do what you like with the material and soar. If you believe in it, then go for it. If you don't then quickly turn the page. Don't let anyone mess with your creativity. This applies to agents, casting directors, and parents of the child too. We suggest you let the child pick which one they like. Give them choices, but please don't make the final decision for them. It will only make them better actors if you give them some freedom.

Sooooo the way into acting is to find the acting map first, the guide the route, the thing called the monologue. It must be the perfect fit or your acting journey will take you out not in. Begin with the right fit and you will end up in a magical place called the heart of acting. A place where you can take pieces of yourself and put them into characters you can relate to, one's you can laugh with, cry with, be scared with or just plain mad at. When you can relate to the character they jump off the page and land right into your heart.

Then the magic begins and the character and the actor come to life to the delight of all.

We hope this book helps you have fun and reach your goals and dreams. Believe in yourself. Always be kind, but don't let anything stand in your way. This is coming from two people that sometimes get so scared we tend to shy away from what we really want and were destined to do. The words have been handed to you. Take them and just go with it. Being an actor isn't always easy, but it's brave and frankly so much fun!!! So go for it, smile and take a chance.

If you don't find what your looking for let us know. Feel free to call or e-mail us. To do so you can go to www.starmapactingschool.com. Remember there is a monologue for you.

Love yourself, love others and embrace your creative soul.

Laurie Ann Davis
Christine Kolenik

# GIRLS: 4-8

# *Rachael*
## (4-8)

My older sister never lets me hang out in our room when her friends are over. She says I'm annoying and not cool enough. Not cool enough? Please! I get all my clothes at Bloomingdales, I was blessed with beautiful hair and I'm the most popular girl in my grade. How much cooler could I be? I mean, what is she talking about? I know I'm two years younger but hanging out with me would really be good for *her*. I'm actually doing her a favor...yeah, that's right I am. You know what? Forget her! I am too great to be brought down by her. Don't you think so teddy? I spend way too much time trying to please her when really I'm about as perfect and as beautiful as you can get! I think I'm gonna ask mom and dad for my own room so I can have my friends over without her being around. Because if you think about it, it's her who isn't cool enough to hang out with me!

# *Christine*
## (4-8)

Sit down kid! I said sit down! I'm going to tell you the truth, something Mom and Dad won't do, but you need to know it. And I'm going to give it to you. You are annoying! You drive me crazy! You're always going in my room, touching all my stuff, going through my drawers, and I can't stand it! You never get in trouble. Mom and Dad like you better and I don't know why! But I'm going to put an end to it. Stop bothering me! Ok you little squirt! You may be my little brother, but you make me so mad I could…. Oh! Stop crying! Shhhhh…stop crying! I'm sorry. Please don't cry, no I didn't mean it. I love you. You're not annoying. You're cute and sweet and well…. I guess I was just jealous. Listen, you stay out of my stuff and I'll promise to play with you everyday for an hour. OK?! Come on, come on you little squirt, let's go color.

# Daureen
## (4-8)

Don't I look pretty? I love clothes. I happen to be very fashionable. I know all the latest styles. You will never catch me wearing something that's not new, hot, now, fresh off the pages of Little Vogue Magazine.

One day I'm going to be the next Tyra Banks, a super model. I will walk down the runway in fashions that I will design myself. The first model who is also a designer. I can see it now, my name in the news my face on TV, bigger than big. Me a Super Model! Look out Tyra, look out Naomi and Cindy here I come.

# *Nicole*
## (4-8)

Everyone thinks I'm cute, sweet, and innocent. They call me cutie, sweetie pie, doll, honey and on and on. Well, I've got news for you. I'm not so sweet. My parents don't know this but I'm known as Knuckles Nicole at school. Cause when I crack my knuckles everyone runs. Relax, I've never hit or pushed or even poked anyone. It's just the sound of my knuckles cracking that gets them scared and running. Can you believe it? I've got the whole school scared of me. Knuckles Nicole and I like it that way. But, keep quiet. Don't tell my parents that their sweetie pie, cutie, doll is really the school bully or you might just be hearing the cracking of knuckles in your future. O.K? Good. See ya.

# *Paxton*
## (4-8)

Leave me alone, just leave me alone. Stop hurting me. You're nothing but a big bully. That's right a bully. You think your so tough pushing around us little kids. Well, it's gonna stop. I told on you. Yeah, that's right I did. The principal, our teacher, my parents, everyone. My parents even called your parents last night. So, it's over. You are in big trouble. By tomorrow we won't have to worry anymore about you. We won't have to be afraid to go to school. Because...Mr. Bully everyone knows your secret. You are a mean nasty boy who is going to be put in a special class away from us.

Yeah, go ahead and cry. Now you know how it feels to be hurt. Not so funny is it?

# *Delores*
## (4-8)


This dress is so ugly Dad! Please talk to Mom. If I wear this for my class picture everyone will make fun of me. What's wrong with it? It has teddy bears on it and it's too big. I'm seven years old. I can't wear a dress like that. I want to wear a dress like a pop star would wear. Something cool! (*pause*) Fine I'll wear that stupid dress and everyone will laugh, but if I have to defend myself and accidentally give someone a black eye or pull hair it will be your fault. You guys will have to get me out of trouble. Now, do you want to re-think making me wear this dress?

# *Jeanie*
## (4-8)

Why would I want to go in the big pool when I can just relax in the kiddie pool? Look at the advantages. I can stand without the water going over my head, no swimmies, no tubes, no kickboards, no pressure! And the best part is I'm the oldest. I can boss everyone around and everyone listens to me and.... ewww gross! Babies in diapers and constant crying. No one my age to play with, and what is that that I just stepped on? Oh my God! I think that kid just peed in the pool. Alright, alright, Mom, I'll learn how to swim. I'll go in the big pool. I won't even hold my nose. Just get me the heck out of here. You just wait, by next week I'll be swimming in the deep end.

# *Emily*
## (4-8)

He loves me, he loves me not, he loves me, he loves me not. He loves me not. He loves me not!! What? I don't believe this. But I love him so much. Silly flower, you can't be right. I take care of him, treat him extra special. I mean I do everything for him. Everything!!! Isn't that right little puppy boy? That flower has to be wrong. Yeah, wrong. I know you love me! I know you do! You cute little puppy.

# BOYS: 4-8

# *Jack*
## (4-8)

Valentine's Day is the worst holiday! My teacher is making us give everyone in class a valentine. How gross!!! I'm a boy. I can't make girly cards with pink hearts. Mom can you help me? If I give cards to the girls in class they will all think that I like them. Jill and Beth already have a crush on me. I can't let them think I like them back! Yuck!! Hey wait…. I know. I'll just put stickers of snakes and bugs on the cards. The girls will scream; boys will laugh; and I can't get in trouble because I gave everyone a card. Problem solved!

# *Billy*
## (4-6)


Mom is the best. She makes me chocolate chip cookies, reads me bedtime stories and buys me lots of toys and takes me to fun places and always makes my boo-boos feel better. I just wish that she would stop calling me Little Peanut. Little Peanut!?! Do I look like a Little Peanut to you? I mean I'm a big boy now. I just wish she would call me Billy or Tough Guy or at least call me Big Peanut. Hey I like that "Big Peanut". What do you think?

# Saverio
## (4-8)

I love Hot Wheels. I collect them. I have hundreds, maybe millions everywhere in boxes, on shelves, in my room, in my den, in the playroom, in my back pack, in mom and dads cars, and even in my desk at school. Every make and color. I have the Bat Mobile, all the X-Men ones, the Spider Man Car, trucks, vans; you name them I got them. I drive my mom crazy, "Put those cars away, somebody is going to trip on them or the dog is going to eat one." One day she'll be sorry. I'm going to build the first giant size Hot Wheels car just like this one and I am going to drive it in the biggest race in the world and I'll win. I'll be known as the Hot Wheel King. Yeah, me a little boy from New York, known as the Hot Wheel King. I just can't wait. I bet Mom can't wait either.

# *Emil*
## (4-8)

I just found out I'm gonna be a big brother. How much does that stink? Now I have to share Mom and Dad. It may not seem so bad to you but listen to this. Now I won't get as many toys at Christmas, I won't have my own room anymore, and no more quiet. All babies do is cry, cry, cry. And the worst part is the baby is going to be a girl. Can you believe that? What can you do with a girl? You can't play ball with a girl. The only thing girls do is complain. I can't stand all the girls in my class. Don't my parents have a clue? Why would they do this? I don't think they thought this whole baby thing through. They really should have talked to me first.

# Patrick
## (4-8)

It felt great, real great! I never thought I could do it. I was so scared but I did it anyway. My mom always says, "Break through the fear," and I did. I'm so glad I took those acting classes. Now, I can say, "I played Charlie in '*Willy Wonka*' at Summit Lane Elementary School." Yeah, me as Charlie! I was a good one too. A star is born

# *Seth*
## (4-8)

I've been waiting all year since the day after last Christmas to get my FAO Schwartz car for this Christmas. I saw it in a magazine and it's all I can think about; dream about. Every Christmas mom and dad always leave our last big present hidden and they give me and my brother clues to find it. And now, finally, I have figured out where it is. Behind this couch is my big, red, beautiful, cool car that only I can drive around the back yard. It's here! I've been waiting 364 long days for it. This is it! I can't wait! Move over world Seth's ready to ride! What!? What the heck is this? This car is remote control! I can't even fit my toe in here. You need a magnifying glass to see it! This must be a joke! It's got to be a joke! I don't feel well. I'm getting dizzy. Gotta sit down. Guess I'll sit on the couch cause, ya know, I can't sit in that tiny thing.

# *Ryan*
## (4-8)

Mom, Dad ...I...well....you see, I really need...boy this is harder than I thought. What I am trying to say is I feel lonely. You know real sad. Friends? I have tons of friends but not a best one and being an only child, well there is no one to play with. You guys are great and all but you're my parents and you can't be everything to me. Don't take this badly but you, you're kind of old. What am I getting at? Well here it goes. Kids need friends, lots of love, something, I mean someone to be with, cuddle with, walk with, Oh, what the....CAN I PLEASE, PLEASE, PLEASE HAVE A DOG?!

# *Matthieu*
## (4-8)

I love my teacher, Mrs. Jones. All the kids say she favors me, and they're right. How can you blame her? I'm good looking, smart, and talented. There really isn't anything bad to say about me. (*pause*) It makes you mad that I think I'm so great? Please, I'm just telling the truth. So as you can see Mrs. Jones is really on top of things.

# *Vincent*
## (4-8)

Sometimes I feel like I don't fit in. I feel different from the other kids. All my friends take karate or play football, baseball or basketball. I like to swim and run but that's it. I don't like sports. Is that weird? I like to listen to music, memorize the words and sing in different voices. I like to dance and pretend I'm different people. Is that wrong? My Dad wants me to sign up for soccer this spring but I want to take an acting class instead. That's where I belong, that's were I will feel like I fit in. Is that bad? I don't think so, do you?

# *Michael*
## (4-8)


I love animals so my parents took me to the Bronx Zoo the other day. We saw lions, tigers and bears. Oh, my! We took a ride on a Camel and saw a bird show. Some of the birds rode bicycles and sang and danced. It was really cool. We saw seals, and sharks and other fish and stuff. My favorite part was the monkey cages. They go crazy and stuff when the people watch them. My Dad kept saying, "Don't get so close. They could grab at you." He must have said it fifty times. He leaned over to look at what kind of monkeys we were looking at. You know, they have these cards in front of the cages that tell you what kind they are. Well, he got too close and one of the monkeys jumped up and grabbed the glasses right off his face. My Dad can't see without his glasses. The rest of the day he thought I was a monkey following him. Poor Dad, he should have taken his own advice. "Don't get to close to the cages."

# GIRLS: 9-13

# Donna
## (9-13)

Remember when you told me I was no good, that I had no talent, that I am a loser and I don't deserve to be the lead in the show? Do you remember? Well I do. I remember how it made me feel. How I cried for days wishing I was anyone else but me. Wondering why you said those things to me and what I had done to make you think that way. Just thought that you might want to know that now I realize why you said those things. It's because you are jealous, and you are cruel. You don't even know me so how could you possibly pass judgement? How could you possibly be so mean? My theory is.....you're just a really angry human being and you took it out on me because I got the role that you wanted. Say what you wanna say and by all means think what you want to think because you are wrong about me. I have talent. I am important and I am going to be whatever I want to be and you'll still be jealous with nothing to show for yourself except a life of coulda, woulda, shoulda's. So you can pretend that you are this nice person to all your friends, and tell yourself how wonderful you are, but I'll always remember what you said to me......and deep down somewhere in that sad soul of yours I know you'll remember too.

# *Lisa*
## (9-13)

I am not going to school tomorrow, or the next day or the next. It was beyond humiliating! And do not tell me to get over it. I will never get over it, and either will the whole school who knows every detail by now.

You can say you called the principal, my teacher, the entire PTA and even the janitor, but it won't make a difference. And how could you even want to send me back to that place? I asked you and Dad to send me to private school and the answer was no, year after year. Well this is what happens when you place your child in a zoo. Don't look at me like that. It is a zoo. Not as nice as the Central Park Zoo or the Bronx Zoo. Oh, no that would be too good for the animals at my school. The animals at my school shouldn't even be called animals. They should be called savages. Yeah, savages!!! Crazy savages who should be hanging from trees and scratching their butts and picking their noses and spreading their toxic waste all over the jungle. But they should not be in school. When will you get it? Public school is for apes not nice young adults who want to learn. I mean think about last year. They stuffed me in a garbage can and you said, "Boys will be boys." The year before that they put dog poop in my locker and you said, "Boys will be boys." Well, Mom today they gave me a wedgy, a big fat wedgy. It took me two hours to get my underwear out of my butt. You can say whatever you want but I am not going back, ever!! Goodnight I am going upstairs to soak my wedgy scars!! Oh, and by the way while I was talking to you "the boys" came up our drive way and spray painted your new Lexus. But oh well, "Boys will be Boys." Right Mom!

# *Barbara*
## (9-13)

A new boyfriend, are you kidding me? I'm only 11 years old and you've already gone through eight so called boyfriends and I've hated them all.

Let's start with Jack. He thought he was my father, bossing me around all the time! Tom, that loser with the fake hair on his head; by the way he was old enough to be your father, and Ralph what a cold fish, he put you down all the time and never wanted me around. Jerry he was young enough to be my brother and used to say "dude" all the time and he called you "Mommy Girl." YUK!! And Ben he was the best. The one who stuttered all the time AAA III WWWOOUULLDD DAHH, it took him fifteen minutes to say I'm going to the bathroom. By the time he got out the words, he ended up peeing in his pants. Come on mom. I can't even remember the other four, I was too young. Please no more boyfriends. How about paying attention to me. Take care of me, your daughter. Spend some time with me. Don't give all your attention to some loser who will never love you more than me. Please no more. Enough already. Please stay home and let's watch a move together ok? Just the girls. Please Mommy don't go. Please....

# *Jolene*
## (9-13)

How dare you! How dare you! Who do you think you are? You come to this town, this school. My town, my school. This has been my home for eleven years. Yeah, that's right. I've been here since the day I was born. This is my home, my territory. Get it. Understand? You're an outsider an army brat, moving from town to town. So don't think you can fly through here for six months or a year and steal all my friends, brown nose my teachers and don't even think about having a crush on my brother. So what am I saying? Don't look so confused. See my face. Pretty angry, huh? Well you ain't seen nothing yet sister. What I'm saying is don't let me see you with my friends, my teacher and especially my brother or I will kick your butt back to Kansas, around to Africa and through Chicago or any of the other places you've lived. Get it? Good. Goodbye! What are you still standing there for? GOOOOO!

# Taylor
## (9-13)

I'm not being a cry baby mom! I really have a bad headache. I'm even seeing spots. Why can't you just once at least pretend to be concerned? I always act tough and I never complain, but sometimes I just want my mommy. Sometimes I want to be babied. What's wrong with that? My whole life you have practically ignored everything that has ever happened to me. When I broke my arm and needed your help with writing my homework you just seemed annoyed. I got no sympathy. And when I had mono, you told me I was being a wimp and you still sent me to school. You make me feel like I have no right to hurt! Well you know what? I can deal with you not caring about the physical things. What hurts the most is when I'm scared or sad and need to talk or just need comfort and you tell me to lighten up. All I want is for you to tell me it's okay. And maybe, if you can spare it....give me a hug. I need you to take care of me. I need you to protect me. You're my mom and it's time you started acting like it!

# Christina
## (9-13)

Oh Mom this is going to be so fun! I am soooo glad that you over looked my behavior last night. I just can't wait to go shopping with you just like you do with Jenny. I know she's older but I can be just as much fun! So how come you are taking me?(*quickly interrupt yourself*) Not that I'm not dying to go! I'm just curious since you always said I wasn't allowed to pick out my own clothes until I'm a teenager. Thanks again for not punishing me for last night!(*pause*) Mom I think you missed the turn to the mall….(*pause*) yeah I am pretty sure that you did! Where the heck are we going? You know I think this is the way too……….oh no! No way, No how! Very funny Mom. Now turn around and go towards the mall. WAIT!!! Why are we stopping? Absolutely not! I am not going into that office. Not unless things have suddenly changed and kids are allowed to give doctors shots. Not the other way around! How cruel! Cruel and unusual punishment. Do you know what that is ma? Cause you should! You wrote the book on it! I am not moving from this car unless there is a big blue sign in front of me that says MALL!! I should have known you would do something like this after I hung up on Jenny's boyfriend last night. I know I told him she was out with someone else but that was a joke…this is not! What? Yearly school physical. Didn't I just get one last year? Fine I'll go but it won't be pretty and I can't promise that Doctor Sorentino won't get something more than a shot from me.

# *Ari*
## (9-13)

I hate history class. Every time the bell rings for fourth period, I want to die. Assigned seats! Assigned seats he gave us! Mr. Urban is a jerk! Why can't we sit where we want? He put me next to Shawn Delaney. You know what he does all fourth period history? He picks his nose! Sometimes he wipes it under his desk and ew....sometimes he eats it!! And with each wipe and each swallow he looks over at me and smiles and says "You want some, Ari?" How gross can you get?!

# *Jeanine*
(9-13)

She didn't mean it Mom.  Chubbs is my nickname.  All my new friends have nicknames that aren't very nice.  I know I haven't known these girls for a long time, but I like them even if you don't.  They invite me places, sit with me at lunch and help me with my make up and clothes so I can look better.  Last weekend Courtney even invited me to sleep over.  Remember?  I am not stupid.  I know you think they use me and pick on me all the time, but that's not true.  I am not the butt of their jokes….(*pause*)  Even if I am….I don't care.  For once I feel like I fit in.  People are paying attention to me.  Whether it's bad or good, at least I'm being noticed.  One minute of not feeling invisible by everyone, including you, is all I ask for.  Look, right now I don't want to hear what you have to say because I really don't care.  I don't want to talk about this anymore.  End of discussion!

# *Maureen*
## (9-13)

That's not me! I'm just not into make up and clothes, cheerleading and boys. I'm not a girly girl! I like sports and video games and dirt. And I really don't like anyone telling me what to do. So why don't you do yourself a favor, stop trying to get me to change my image, (*make quotation sign with fingers*) and focus on this project. Gosh, it's bad enough we have to work together. Do you really need to keep yap yap yappin' away? You just keep decorating and I will look up the info...(*silence*) What!? Oh just shut up! Why are you trying to talk and be friends with me anyway? We're different. You have your friends and I have mine. I hate to burst your cheery, school spirity, pink bubble but not everyone has to get along. I'm not gonna change. Most people don't. That's what it's like in the real world, so do yourself another favor and start getting used to it.

# *Brittany*
## (9-13)

That's it! You have said enough. I am through putting up with you and... I am not some piece of garbage you can push around. Yeah, I may be only 11 but I've been through a lot. I've met girls like you before. You think you're tough, cool, smart, ALL THAT. Well...you're not tough, cool, or smart. As a matter of fact you are the dumbest person I have ever met!! And I am going to put a stop to your bullying. See I'm on top now, not you! I may be the new kid in town but you're all washed up. So move along and find some new helpless defenseless kid to spread rumors about. Go ahead and try!!!

I'll be watching you and your so-called friends. Oh...by the way, you know why you are the way you are? You know why you do the things you do? Yeah, come closer. Closer, I have a secret that can save your parents a lot of money on therapy. See I got the answer right here. You say things that aren't true about other kids because you're afraid, (*laughing*) yeah afraid. You're not a bully after all...you're a scaredy cat...meow...you're jealous. See, you want to be like me and those innocent kids you make fun of.

Well I got news for you. I like who I am and you know what? Jealousy will get you nowhere fast. So bye, bye...I gotta go now see I am on the way up and...as for you...enjoy the flight down.

# *Kylie*
## (9-13)

How dare you talk to me that way! I'm not some idiot you can push around. You think you are so cool, but your not. Everyone is laughing behind your back, even your friends. Don't look so shocked. Yeah every one of them. Being captain of the cheerleading squad doesn't give you the right to talk down to us. Take a look at yourself. Get yourself some help. Why don't you just stop acting like an idiot and stop torturing us. Get a life and maybe we just might hang with you again. Until then get lost.

# *Dana*
## (9-13)

This stinks! Who thought of this anyway? I mean what am I dog or something? Hello! I am a kid not an animal. Better yet I'm not a captive slave. Do this, do that. Any other commands you have for me? I mean I go to school all week, come home and do homework, set the table for dinner, clean the table after the dinner, take a shower, lay out my clothes for the next day and then I wake up, make my bed, make my own breakfast and get myself on the bus. Don't you think on the weekends I could just lay around and watch television? No I have to shovel cow poop into your garden so you can have nice flowers. Must I repeat myself? When do I get a break? When is it my day?

# *Monica*
## (9-13)

When am I gonna learn? When? Obviously never mom so you might as well realize this and stop wasting your time trying to figure out new ways to ground me, cause there pretty much isn't anyway that you can stop me! I know that it's destructive but its fun! And seeing the look on Alice's face is worth just about anything you might threaten to do to me. I mean come on. Don't you think that maybe you should be having a talk with Alice? I do this to her once every couple of months, you'd think that she would know that by now. I think she may be a little slow. All these boyfriends are taking up way to much room in her head; and let's face it there wasn't too much room to begin with! Alright, alright I promise I'll stop saying mean things about her but she's my older sister; it comes with the territory. If she wasn't so evil to me maybe I wouldn't put blue hair dye in her shampoo.(*pause*) Now, back to your original question. When am I gonna learn? I have learned. I've learned that it really makes my sister mad when her hair turns blue right before a date. And that's a great way to get back at her when she's mean to me! The question you should be asking is when is she gonna learn.

# *Patricia*
## (9-13)

You are so annoying! This conversation is so annoying! I can't listen to you anymore. Why is it that every time I get a bad grade or get in trouble in school you find it necessary to announce to Mom and Dad how you always got A's and never had detention even once? Do you really think I care about what you did? Grades and school really don't mean that much to me. I have other interests. I am my own person and I am so sick and tired of you trying to make me feel bad for who I am. Well guess what.........I *don't* feel bad. Why should I? To please you? That's the difference between us you know. I don't spend my life worrying about what other people think. Maybe if you didn't spend so much time caring about the way I act, I would stop trying to act the exact opposite of you. Because you know what? I'm not like you and I never will be. I realize that and accept it. Maybe its time you did too!

# *Adrianna*
## (9-13)

I can't believe they won't let me go. Are they kidding me? I mean what's the big deal. They are so paranoid. Nothing is going to happen to me. They act as if someone will kidnap me or something. It's not like I'm going to be alone. Emily's Mom will be with me the whole time. What ever happened to the meaning of the word guardian? It's as if I asked to go to Iraq for a vacation. She's a bad influence my Mom says. She has inappropriate behavior my dad says. She's no role model my mom says. They are making such a big deal over nothing. I just want to go and have fun. It's just a Brittany Spears concert. It's not like I'm going to see Madonna or something.

# *Eileen*
## (9-13)

Tap, tap, back and left and right, twist and....what the heck? (*to the "person" next to you*) Do you have any idea how to do this?..... ugggg when is this gonna be over? Thank goodness....finished! (*follow the "person" to the fourth wall*) I can't believe my mom made me take this class. It's ridiculous don't you think? I mean how does this teacher expect us to follow what she's doing when she goes so fast and moves her body so awkwardly? There has to be something seriously wrong with her. I don't think a person's legs are supposed to do that but...that's just me. Do you agree? (*wait for answer*) No........ okay well I could tell that you got the hang of this whole thing a little more than me, but still, come on? Your mom must be forcing you to do this too right!? (*wait*) Your mom isn't forcing you? Your mom's the teacher....huh.....boy did I just put my big uncoordinated foot in my mouth. But...a....you know I was kidding about the teacher, I mean your mom having serious problem right!? Clearly I meant I had serious problems because I can't do the steps and your mom explains them so well and...huh? What the....where did she go? Did I say something wrong? It's time to talk to my mom about a new hobby. I don't think this ones working out.

# Dawn
## (9-13)

Can you believe she had the nerve to say that about me? Who does she think she is? How could she spread rumors that aren't true? Now everyone thinks I did it. Everybody. I can't even walk down the hall without hearing giggles and whispers. Pointing, yes they are even pointing at me. My face was five shades of red all day. I can't get away from it. How dare she ruin my life like this? I am not guilty. There is no way I would ever kiss Michael Clinton behind the school or anywhere else for that matter. He's cute and all but, Gross!

# *Morgan*
## (9-13)

He is so hot. I can't take it. What is wrong with me? I have no control. Every time I see him I freak. I get all giggly and weird. I can't stop myself. I start to sweat and I feel like I'm going to throw up. I've never felt this way before. I mean I had a crush on Paul, Robert and Hugh but it was different. I mean my feelings for them lasted only three or four weeks and I didn't have trouble talking to them, but this hottie just makes me weak in the knees. Oh my God, I think he's the one. The one I'm going to fall in love with. My first love. He's my first love; yeah that's it. Now all I have to do is get him to notice me.

# BOYS: 9-13

# *Rob*
## (9-13)

I'm thinking cool it's almost summer time. My parents can't afford to send me to camp but that's o.k. We got a pool, a big back yard and well there is always the beach, the park, other activities, no prob. Then my Mom lays it on me. She says, "Your cousin Sammy is going to spend the summer with us." I am like "What?" "Sammy, slow, fat, big round stupid Sammy." That kid is no relation of mine. He is more like the cousin of Patrick Star from Sponge Bob. "Duh, my name is Sammy and I am an idiot and I am fat and pick my nose all day and when I jump in the pool all the water spills out over the side, Duh!!" There goes my summer. I say "Mom are we talking all summer?" She tells me that Sammy's parents are going through a bad divorce and Sammy needs a break from all the craziness. He needs a break, what about me? I am the one who is going to be tortured all summer. This kid is insane, I kid you not. Sammy is the most annoying person you will ever meet on the planet. And another thing he tells lies, he lies about everything and the worst part is my parents always believe him. Last year at Christmas all the cookies were gone before dinner and he told everyone it was me and they believed him. I got sent to my room without dessert while that loser ate even more food, like he needs it. Everyone feels sorry for him because he is a loser, so he gets away with murder while I suffer. Hey, I appreciate that my Mom and Dad are nice people and want to help Sammy out but does it have to be at my expense. And whatever happened to not having enough money for summer camp? It's going to cost a million dollars just to feed that kid for two months. Looks like my summer's over even before it begins. Thanks Mom, thanks Dad. Thanks a lot.

# Jim
## (9-13)

Listen Mr. Gold, I'm really a very charming guy and this was all a terrible misunderstanding, and I really shouldn't be here in the principal's office. Ms. Victor left the room for a minute to take Amy to the nurse….really that girl is such a klutz….and she asked us to please behave while she was gone. Since no one was listening I simply tried to control the class, to help Ms. Victor of course, by doing a few Jim Carrey impressions….(*actor does an impression*). Do you see the stunning resemblance? We even have the same first name. (*pause*) Okay, guess not. Anyway, the point is I was merely trying to help not distract. It was an accident when I hit the globe, which knocked over the lizard tank, which set the lizards free. It's not my fault all the girls started screaming. You don't look so happy. You know, I think Ms. Victor has a thing for you. You can tell by the way she gives you "the eyes." Can you blame her? You're really a great guy. So what do you say? You gonna let this one slide? (*pause*) Yup…didn't think so. See you in detention.

# *Tommy*
## (9-13)

I hate her. I'm sorry but I don't care if it's not nice to say "I hate her." The minute I laid my eyes on her I hated her. Pure hate! I did what you said and gave her a chance. As a matter of fact I gave her a million chances. I work my butt off to please her and I try to find things to like about her, despite the fact that she smells, has a mole on the tip of her nose the size of Texas and that she has a five o'clock shadow at 8 a.m. I've overlooked all that but all I get are B's and C's when I'm doing A quality work. It's been two months and I still feel the same way. So now help me out Mom and get me out of Mrs. Davis's class tomorrow or I'll never go to school again.

# Dennis
## (9-13)

Embarrassing? Last night crossed the line of embarrassing. You would not believe what my dad did. Actually if you knew my dad or even met him for one second you would believe it. Anyway last night was the Blink 182 concert. Since my dad doesn't think my friends and I are old enough to go alone, he *volunteered* to chaperone us, which frightened me cause my dad loves making a fool of himself in front of my friends. So its 6:30…all my friends are at my house ready to go and out of his bedroom walks; or should I say skateboards my dad. You wouldn't believe it!!! He was wearing ripped jeans, a black Blink 182 t-shirt that he cut so you could see his stomach and he dyed his hair green. My father had green spiked hair!!! I wanted to die! My Mom was laughing and my friends were frozen in shock. And to top off my embarrassment, the first thing he said was, "ready for the far out concert dudes? Maybe we'll see some hot chicks. Far out!? Who says that anymore? The man thinks he's hilarious. I was completely mortified the whole night while my Dad had the time of his life. What is wrong with him? What planet did he come from? You know what's scary? He does this stuff all the time! God, is it possible to put your parents up for adoption?

# *Deric*
## (9-13)

Oh man, I totally forgot that my book report is due today. Stupid book report! What am I gonna do? I can't tell the teacher that I didn't read the book and don't have a speech prepared. I've got to think of something. Maybe I can fake being sick. Yeah, good idea Deric!!! Hmmm...how about chicken pocks? No, that won't work. I don't have any red spots on me. What about a stomach ache? Nah, too common, and everyone will know something's up. Wait! I know! What about laryngitis? It's perfect! If I have laryngitis I can't talk, and if I can't talk then I can't possibly give a speech about my book. Phew...what a relief. Sometimes, I really think I'm too smart for my own good. I better check my homework sheet so I know what's due tomorrow and I don't forget my homework again. Let's see...Wednesday I have a math test and (*cut yourself off*)...wait a minute! Today is Wednesday.....aw geez, today is our math test not our book report. And you don't need to speak to take a math test. Guess laryngitis can't get me out of this one.

# *Vince*
## (9-13)

Someone needs to tell me what the heck is going on with my sister. Earlier she was in the bathroom with my mom and they were both crying. My Dad was standing outside the door asking if my sister was okay every five seconds saying, "My daughter's not a little girl anymore." And I was being told to go to my room and play video games. Well excuse me for wanting to know what all the commotion was about. Sorry for being a little confused about why, when my sister finally came out of the bathroom she was waddling around, and she looked like she had a diaper on. So I asked my mom why all of a sudden she looked like Donald Duck. I'm not completely sure what she said back to me. I couldn't make out her words because she was yelling at me so loud. I think she said something about how I should be sensitive to the changes my sister was going through. And I am positive that somewhere between the high pitched screeching I was told that I better be nice to my sister and leave her alone if I ever wanted to play my Play Station again. Boy there's a lot of chaos when girls get older. I just hope I don't look like Goofy when I turn thirteen.

# Nicholas
## (9-13)

I can't help it Mom! You would be pouting too! You know I hate doing this. Why couldn't you just leave me in the car? What boy likes to go with their Mom to the nail place? This is embarrassing and it's for girls. No, I never watch ma, I always just sit and look out the window. I don't need to see you get a pedigree, petacue, peta whatever they do to your toenails. (*pause*) All right if I turn around and look will you leave me alone? Good! (*pause*) Hey what are they doing to your feet? They're rubbing and cleaning and.....huh? You get to put them in warm water with bubbles? Why didn't you tell me you don't have to put a color on your toes? Jeez ma, you could have saved a lot of time for yourself and I wouldn't have to be so bored. Hey Mom can you make me an appointment for tomorrow? I could really use one of those after my soccer game.

# *Vito*
## (9-13)

I don't want to play basketball, football, baseball, soccer or any sport for that matter. I hate sports and the only reason I played any of them was because you wanted me to. But that's not what I want to do. Don't you understand that? I want to act. I want to sing. I want to see my name in big bright lights on Broadway. I want to star in a movie with Brittany Murphy and have everyone be in love with me. But that's not manly enough for you is it Dad? That would make you ashamed of me? It would be embarrassing for you to tell people that you are going to see your son act in a play and not score the winning touchdown in a football game. Just so you are aware, I hear you talk to Mom. I hear what you say about me. I'm a sissy, wimp, a disappointment amongst other mean things. Well that stuff hurts. You should love and be proud of me because I am your son, no matter what I want to do. I love you, and am proud of you even though you don't make a lot of money or own your own business. I love you because you are my Dad and the rest of that stuff doesn't matter to me. I love you because you are you, so please support me whether I want to be quarterback of a super bowl team or the lead in the next Neil Simon play.

# *Bobby*
## (9-13)

What are you looking at? You stare at me all the time like I'm an alien from outer space. Day in and day out, stare, stare. Do you have any idea how that makes me feel? You've been staring at me since school started. That's (*counts on fingers*) nine months. I am going crazy. Either you knock it off or else I'm gonna stare at you (*stare at him*). How does that feel? Not too good I bet. (*keeps staring*) Well, I am going to keep it up for the next nine months every time I see you, or maybe I'll do it even longer. Yeah, I will do it longer and then maybe after you've gone crazy I'll stop. But until then I am gonna stare, stare, stare at you so you will know what it feels like. And then maybe just maybe you'll never do it to anybody else again. Got it! Good. (*stares*)

# Roy
## (9-13)

Please stop hurting me. I can't take it anymore. I'm going crazy. Do you understand? If you don't stop, I'm going to tell. I will tell everyone, my Mom, Dad, sisters, the principal of the school and all my friends. You'll go to jail. You can say what you want but I'm thirteen years old and I know better now. I'm not eight years old. You can't tell me to keep it a secret anymore. I'm not afraid of you. I know you can't hurt my parents. They can hurt you and so can I. And I'm going too. Right now. It's over.

# *Paul*
# (9-13)

We used to go to this park. I was real little so I don't remember the name of it, but it was the biggest park I have ever seen. It went on for miles and miles. And it was amazing, the brightest green grass you have ever seen and flowers everywhere. We would go on these trails and walk for hours. I never got tired because there was so much to see and discover. Every time we saw something different, chipmunks, black squirrels, lizards, and more.

The best part of those days at the park was the talks we had underneath the coolest tree. It must have been a hundred feet tall or more and it had this one branch that bent down like a swing and she used to put me on it and swing me back and forth. I know it's not reality to think that only we knew about that tree and only we sat and talked under it for hours but that's how it felt. I learned about life under that tree; life the way it was and way it is and even the way it's going to be. See, I learned it from this magical woman who took me on those adventurous walks and with whom had those endless talks. She taught me how to be a good young man a courageous and strong young man. One who will make a difference. That park and that tree will always be the place I will go when I'm happy and when I am sad and it will be the place that I will take my son when it's time to tell him about life and the magical woman who brought me here; my grandma. I'll miss you grandma. Sweet dreams. May you forever swing on the tree in peace.

# TEEN GIRLS: 14-18

# *Caroline*
## (14-18)

You will never believe this. What I am about to tell you is going to blow your mind. I can't even believe it myself. So far everyone I told thinks I am totally lying. They think I am just one big fat liar. Not that I'm fat or anything, you know that's just a saying. Big Fat Liar. Where did that come from anyway? Big Fat Liar. It makes no sense unless you really are fat and a liar. Well, we already made it clear that I am not FAT and I am definitely not a liar. What was I talking about? Oh, yeah! Oh, my god. You will never believe what happened to me. I went on that audition yesterday for that new reality show they're doing in Manhattan. It wasn't really an audition, they just talked to me and asked me questions. It was one of those things, either they want you or they don't. It's not based on talent or anything. Well, anyway they make small talk and then say, "We'll call your agent." Yeah, right sure you will, I don't even have an agent. I then proceed to walk out and I head down the hallway of Fox Studios and all of the sudden I see this guy who is dressed like a homeless person. He's got on an old wool hat, a flannel shirt, you know the kind an old construction worker wears and dirty old boots with jeans that look like they were taken out of a Salvation Army bin and never washed. Gross! There is nobody else in the hallway but me and this guy and he is defacing public property. He is standing in front of an old poster of that Television show that was popular in the 80's or 90's, Twenty One Jump Street. The guy has the glass off the poster and is making devil horns and mustaches on Holly Robinson and some of the other characters. I know I should have walked away, considering I was afraid. But I said "Hey, do you know you are defacing public property and you could go to jail for that." His back was to me and he just said "Yeah." And then he said "Can you help put this glass back on the poster?" I said, "I certainly will not, then I could get in trouble." Then all of the sudden he turns around and guess who it is? Guess? (*she squeals*) JOHNNY DEPP. JOHNNY DEPP. I swear on my life. I say, "You're Johnny Depp" as I proceeded to help him put the glass back on. "I can't believe I'm helping Johnny Depp commit a crime." And I am screaming. (*she screams to demonstrate*) He said, "What do I have to do to keep you quiet? What do you want? I'll give you anything to keep you quiet." I was stunned, and then I said, "I'll take your autograph." "No problem," he said and proceeded to write on the envelope that I had my headshots in. Then he says, " I can't believe that's what you asked for." "What should have I asked for?" I said. He said in that smooth Johnny Depp voice with his beautiful eyes twinkling, "Well," he said "anything, you could have asked for. A car, a house and you know some girls would have asked for a kiss or something." As he said this he started to head down the long hallway. I yelled, "Hey wait, I changed my mind, I'll take that kiss." He just waved and kept on walking. Can you believe it I met Johnny Depp? See you don't believe it do you? I did and what an idiot. I asked for an autograph when I could have got a kiss. What? A car, a house? You sound like my parents. They said the same thing. Who care's about that stuff when you could get kiss from JOHNNY DEPP. ( *she screams*) I met Johnny Depp. I met Johnny Depp.

# Shannon
## (14-18)

Today was definitely the most embarrassing day of my life. I'm sitting in Math class, barely paying attention and Ms. Lambert calls on me. Just as I was about to say, "I'm sorry can you repeat the question," I farted (*quietly with a look of disgust*)....and it was so loud I think the whole school shook. I couldn't even attempt to pretend that it wasn't me. The whole class started laughing except for Scott Prestly, the hottest guy in school. The love of my life! He sits right behind me and instead of laughing he started coughing. He was coughing so hard I think he began to choke. I didn't know what to do. Even Ms. Lambert was grossed out. Word got around school so fast. Everyone that walked by me called me *stink bomb*. I couldn't wait for school to be over. I was mortified! To top things off, next Friday is the school dance and I have been dreaming about going with Scott and how we would be crowned king and queen of the dance. Now he'll never ask me to go....and the only thing I'll be queen of is letting it rip in Math class.

# *Krista*
## (14-18)

He is so hot. I mean HOT!!! Incredibly hot. Tall and ripped, nice and lean. Like a fine cut of beef. Delicious. His eyes are like dark rich chocolate brownies and he has the best ass I have ever seen. The minute I laid eyes on him I thought, MMMmm what a man. What a very fine man. Girl, everyone had their eye on him but I got him. Yeah, I got him. He took one look at me and our eyes locked; we became one. Boy if my Mom and Dad knew, they'd kill me. Every Monday and Saturday I told my Mom that I had cheerleading practice and I'd meet him down by the school. We would take off in his car and explore and have fun. We went to the beach, down to the lake and took many trips into Manhattan. I can't tell you how many Broadway shows I've see. The worst part is I can't talk about them. Did you ever see Wicked? Wow it was amazing. My mom loves musicals, I wanted to tell her so bad but I couldn't. I wanted to say Mom I just saw the best Broadway musical with the hottest, nicest guy. But I couldn't, she and my father would have had me committed, locked up, chained to anything metal. It's funny, they say to be truthful to your parents but you can't be because if you do they will say no. They'll say no to everything, anything that you want to do or have. But I wish I could have told Mom about Mr. Wonderful. I guess if I did she would have said "Are you crazy, he's twice your age, old enough to be your father." She would have turned twenty different shades of red and then locked me in my room. Well, I sure do wish I did tell her and well, I wouldn't be here now if I did. *(Opens up her coat to reveal a pregnant belly)*

# *Charlene*
## (14-18)

I don't want to go to bed Mom. I want to tell you something. You keep on trying to avoid the subject and it's making me really mad. I know you think I'm just a kid and I was too young to know what was going on between you and Dad, but I thought I would let you know that you couldn't be more wrong. I knew exactly what was happening. Do you really think I couldn't hear the screaming, the loud noises, you crying hysterically? I used to put my ear right up against your door every night so I could hear what was going on. So I would know if you were ok, or if I needed to get help, or if dad hit you so hard that he knocked you over and you hit your head. You can try to deny it like you always have. You were good at pretending and fake smiling, but the bruises didn't lie. When I found you early that Monday morning before school I thought you were dead and that I would be alone without you for the rest of my life. And every day since that Monday even though dad is gone I am so scared that I will walk down those stairs and find you lying there again. That's why I am always late in the morning. It's why I never want to go anywhere without you and it's why I'm always having nightmare's and screaming your name in my sleep. I'm not asking you to tell me that everything is gonna be ok. I just want you to talk to me and let me know what's going on. And please tell me when you speak to dad because I am scared that you will take him back without telling me first. Atleast give me the comfort of a warning so next time I can prepare to be alone.

# *Stefanie*
## (14-18)

I was so looking forward to school this year. I know, me looking forward to school is completely unheard of. But they added Dramatic Arts to the curriculum. Finally, I'm a senior and they decide to add it, when I've wanted it since seventh grade. I still have to deal with Earth Science and Math but I figure I could get through this last year if I take Drama. I've always wanted to be an actor so now I finally get my chance to learn all about acting. Well I get to the auditorium early because I'm so excited and of course every loud-mouthed thespian is there. I know I've been in the same school with these kids for the past five years but I don't recognize one of them. Of course they're all clicky and jumping all over each other. I think half of them are gay, not that that matters but it was kind of grossing me out. But anyway, I kept saying to myself "Just ignore it, just ignore them, you really want to do this so just keep focused." Finally in walks the teacher and she looks like she's eighteen. I look older than her. I think she said she was twenty-five or six. Well anyway, she's all bubbly and hyperactive like a kid who just chased three candy bars with a liter of Pepsi. "She's like hi, name is Miss Gillmore, but everybody calls me Gilly." Is she kidding me, Gilly? "Welcome to Dramatic Arts, we are going to have a lot of fun" "Please know that I am very excited to be your teacher and hope to make your acting journey a pleasant one." O.K., not good. I'm hating her already. I'm thinking she is definitely a left over high school cheerleader who got an acting degree, never went out and auditioned or got a job and finally has her first acting gig trying to act like a high school dramatic arts teacher who knows how to teach. If she can pull this off she should get a Tony, an Oscar, Golden Globe, SAG award, and an Emmy. It only got worse, we proceeded to spend the next hour taking turns pretending to be flowers as each student one at time got the opportunity to pick one of us. "Smell the flowers, feel the grass, notice the trees, what beautiful flowers they are." I wanted to throw up. Well, I guess you figured I'm not going back. The woman is an idiot. That's about the only award she will ever win; The IDIOT AWARD. And as for the school, what were they thinking? There goes my opportunity to learn about acting. No, I take that back I'm going to find a better teacher. Bye-Bye Gilly!

# *Julia*
## (14-18)

People think I am too young to have this problem. My parents were in complete denial. They kept sending me to doctors, insisting that I had some sort of unknown disease that was causing me to lose weight. What they didn't understand is that I did.......I do have a disease and it's called anorexia. I'm honestly not sure exactly when it started. I just know I have felt fat my whole life. I can remember being little and everyone calling me the funny, chubby one and my sister the pretty one. I was fat and she was thin and that was always made known to me. I remember one Christmas when I was 8 and she was 10 and my parents got my sister ballet classes and me cooking classes. I was devastated and completely jealous. I wished that for once everyone would see me as this beautiful ballerina with the perfectly skinny body. Then one day before I knew it, I got my wish. I became that ballerina.....I became obsessed. I ate practically nothing and would throw away food when my parents weren't looking. It's all I thought about. Every morning the first thing I would do is weigh myself and after each pound was lost all I wanted to do was lose more. It was never enough. I'm not even in high school yet and I've lost chunks of my hair and I have an irregular heart beat from all the damage I have done to my body....(*pause*) So now after a lot of hard work I am slowly getting better. Slowly trying to be happy and healthy again. Slowly being able to have dreams beyond that damn ballerina.

# *Nancy*
## (14-18)

(*Holding a guitar, awkwardly strumming it*) I always wanted to take guitar lessons. I love the sound they make. (*Strums the guitar*) Guitars are so cool. I picture myself on stage one day singing a song I wrote. Not a real big stage, something intimate like the Beacon, Westbury Music Fair or The Downtown. Just me and my guitar singing my songs to the audience who love my music and me. It is so cool that my parents got me this guitar for my birthday. My dad has said no to guitar lessons for over a year now. I wonder what made him change his mind. Well, who cares as long as he said yes. I started lessons yesterday. They brought me into this little room with just two chairs and told me to wait for the instructor. I was so nervous. About three minutes later, in walks this guy wearing a black baseball hat, with a tight tee-shirt on. My mouth just hung open. He has to be the cutest, hottest guy I have ever seen. I wanted to die. He sits down next to me in that other chair which is on top of me and says "Hi, my name is Jesse and I'm going to be your teacher, I hope that's o.k. with you?" I'm thinking okay are you kidding me? How am I supposed to focus on taking guitar lessons when you're in the room, Jesse? I'm like there goes my dream of being a guitar player; my dreams of being on stage, gone. All I could think of was, I'm in love. He takes out my guitar and says "Wow a Taylor, awesome." And I say, "No, my name is Nancy." What an idiot. My name is Nancy? He says, "No, I meant the guitar, it's a Taylor, they're the best, they've got a great sound." I wanted to die. I didn't even know my guitar had a name. No wonder my Dad said no to lessons, I'm an idiot. Who knew guitars have names. So, there he is my guitar in hand and he starts to play it. It starts to get real hot in the room and then he starts to sing. He had the most beautiful voice I ever heard. And like a complete idiot I gush "You should be famous."

What a dork. He just laughed the cutest laugh I ever heard in my life with his pearly white teeth sparkling up against the lights. I thought I died and went to hotty heaven. He then proceeds to show me hand positions on the guitar. Get this he stands behind me and puts his arms around me like this (*demonstrates*) and takes my hands and places them into position like this and what do you think I do? I start laughing and I say "That tickles." The lesson was only ½ hour and it went way too fast. He gave me some chords to work on C, G and F. Well I can't wait to go back for my next lesson and I think I already wrote my first song. (*She sings and strums the three chords, Jesse, Oh Jesse I think I'm in love with you*)

# *Karen*
## (14-18)

I can't help it! It's not like I do it on purpose or anything. Some things just can't be controlled. My body just freaks out. My mind goes off into this weird zone or something. Not something you could describe to someone, not out loud at least. I know I'm not making any sense. It's just how I get through the day; every day. I hate school. Please don't look so shocked. It is an awful place. No one even likes each other. And well, they all hate me for sure. Please understand that when I do it I am still able to learn and get good grades. I mean my last report card proves that, well except for the C in Math. But I will get a B next time, I promise. You can't do anything anyway. You would have to take out a piece of my brain to stop it and well, I'm sure you don't want to do that. Do you?? You do? What? How could you even think it? See, we're different! We've always been different. Is it possible I was adopted? Or am I just a freak of nature. I'm not like Dad either. Both of you always do the right thing all the time. You are both so smart and organized. That can't be fun by the way. Me I am just a mess and messy. One big garbage bag filled with the stuff people just don't need anymore. I'm like one big thrift shop stuffed into a young woman's body; a lost person with two parents who think she's nuts. Well, I guess you are just going to have to get rid of me cause I just can't stop. It's what I do and I will continue to do it for the rest of my life. It feels good. You and Dad will just have to except it; except me for who I am. A day dreamer that's what I am, a creative soul who just can't stop dreaming dreams. Mom it's not so bad to have one for a daughter. It's not like it hurts anybody or anything. Try it sometime. Dream a little dream. It feels good, really it does.

Just close your eyes and think of somewhere you really want to go or something you really want. Don't be afraid to dream. You know what Mom if you dream hard enough and often, I bet your dream will come true. Come on mom, you can tell me. What is it that you want? There's got to be something! Everybody wants something! Everybody has at least one dream!

# Kathleen
## (14-18)

I want to do it all the time. It makes me feel good. I know it's wrong but school is such a hassle. I can't seem to make the grade and my home life sucks. My Mom and Dad don't even know I exist. Between the two of them they work over a hundred hours a week and when they're not at work, they're at the club or some meeting. The worse part is that they don't even spend time with each other. It's not like I can say my parents at least have a good marriage. They ignore me, each other, the house, the dog and the exotic fish they bought. I spend every day and night by myself. If I eat one more frozen dinner I think I'll puke. So getting high is all I have. It makes me feel good. I get to laugh for a few hours. It's my home away from home. It's the only home I know. The only home I feel comfortable in. "The house of weed."

# *Jenna*
## (14-18)

Quiet, Shhh, Quiet. Do you hear it? No? Are you really listening? You can't be really listening if you don't hear it. I think that 98% of the population doesn't really listen. I mean, they don't really listen to sounds. They may hear words now and then like: "Would you like something to eat?" "Do you need any money?" "Can I do something for you?" "Do you want to step all over me and use me and then throw me away?" Yeah, they hear things like that maybe but not true sounds, sounds of the soul. Listen, I'm not crazy, I'm just telling the truth. The only sounds people may hear are the loud sounds of thunder and lightening or an explosion and fear that they may get hurt so they need time to run. Or people will respond to sounds that scare them or maybe jump when someone says BOO. But that's about it. They're limited on their sound intake. One night I was lying in my bed and I couldn't sleep. It was about two o'clock in the morning and I hear this tiny cry. First I thought I was imaging it, dreaming with my eyes open. But it wasn't just my imagination, I heard it and it sounded as if it was coming from outside. I went downstairs and walked into the kitchen and it became louder. I went back to my Mom and Dad's bedroom to tell them I heard a noise and they came into the kitchen concerned and checked out the house, the backyard, everywhere. My Dad said, "Go back to sleep you're hearing things." I went back to bed and as soon as I laid down I heard it again. I got dressed and went out into the backyard myself. I was scared. I knew I heard a tiny cry and I had to see what it was. Sure enough, under the big tree in the back of my yard was a tiny black kitten; couldn't have been more then two or three weeks old. It was the cutest kitten I had ever seen. I took it in and gave it warm milk with an eyedropper and wrapped it in a blanket. I held it all night. His name is Sounds. It may be a strange name but I like it. See if we all listened, really listened we could hear the sounds of people's hearts beating, racing, feeling, crying out. The sounds you don't usual hear are the important ones. The ones we need to listen too. Cause if you really listen you just may find out what someone is really saying, feeling, wanting. Like Sounds my kitten just wanted to be rescued, held, loved, and to be taken care of. That's all, that's all he wanted. Sounds are a great thing aren't they?

# *Lauren*
## (14-18)

Oh my God!! Oh my God!! My Mom comes into my room Friday with my Dad no less and they both sit on either sides of my bed. Picture this…, there I am, walkman on full blast rocking out to Eminem and they have these looks on their faces like someone died. I am like what's up? They stare at me with these looks and then my mom hands me this pamphlet that has girls dancing through daisies on it. I stare back at them and my Mom says, "Honey, every woman needs to maintain her health," and then my father says, "You are at the age when it is time to see a Gynecologist" Gross!! I must see a Gyno what? My mom says, "He is a doctor who specializes in," and get this, she whispers …."vaginas." And my Dad says "And bosoms too and so much more." I wanted to die and I am like what does this have to do with me? You have an appointment tomorrow they tell me with Dr. Manning. "No way," I say. "Yes" they say, "There is no choice Lauren." Well, I go alright and meet this so called Dr. Manning and he is this short, bald really really old guy. He is about 40 and every time he talks spit lands on his lips and sometimes in your face and every two seconds he says, " Do you understand what I am saying?" And his eyes blink about a million times when he says it. O.K. then they put me in this disgusting white gown and tell me to take everything off and put my feet in stirrups like a saddle or something, only I am not riding any horse. He then proceeds to grope my breasts and as he is doing it he asks what my favorite movies are and I am like are you kidding me? Next he holds up these metal claps that look like Donald Ducks mouth and he says, "Relax, we are going to insert these into your vagina" and I'm like my WHAT?!?. No way is that gonna fit. Maybe you have something in a Hughy, Dewy or Louie size. He laughs and more spit comes out. Now, I am thoroughly grossed out. He says, "Just Relax, pant like a puppy and everything will be alright" Well, after the exam he actually tries to shake my hand. Are you kidding me? That is the last time I am going to pant like a puppy or put my feet in any kind of stirrups; horse or no horse!

# *Joanne*
## (14-18)

I spent months looking for my dress. I wanted the perfect one. I got my hair, nails and make-up done at Marcucc For Hair, my favorite salon in Malvern. I wanted everything to be perfect. My parents even let me get my hair colored and my teeth whitened. My parents were great. They understood how important this night was too me. This dress is designer you know. It was beautiful. They put fresh flowers in my hair. My favorite flowers, gardenias. I love the smell of gardenias, so pure and sweet. But not anymore the smell makes me sick to my stomach. I feel like I'm going to throw up. Its o.k., don't, no please don't I want to talk. I want to get it over with. It was the most amazing night, clear sky filled with stars, the weather perfect, and a cool breeze on a Friday night, the luckiest night of my life. I mean, the most popular boy in school asked me to the prom. I mean I'm pretty well liked but I don't mix with that crowd, the cool crowd, the crowd that makes our hall ways part like the red sea when they walk down it. But he asked me. At first I thought it was a joke. He said he always admired me and thought I was smart, different from the rest of the girls. Mature he said, he said I was mature. I didn't look into it or anything, I just couldn't believe that Jimmy Doyle was asking me to the prom. I mean he's gorgeous; every girl in the school wants him. Even the teachers melt when he's in their presence. He's smart too. We have been in history class for the past three years together and his grades are just below mine. We recently had to do a project in Mr. Whitby's class on our favorite president and we had a contest on who could find out the most facts about the president we picked and I won and Jimmy came in second place. The winner got this cute trophy and a gift certificate to the mall. I didn't realize Jimmy was such a sore loser. He said he wanted to win, he needed to win that stupid little trophy and gift certificate and that no girl should make him look bad. So he took me to the prom to humiliate me. He could just not have showed up or left me at the prom and went home, but did he have to brutalize me and ra......me, tear my beautiful designer dress. Couldn't he just have not ever showed up, just not picked me up? Leave me at door wondering? That would have been humiliating enough, don't you think?

# *Victoria*
## (14-18)

It feels good. Real good. Like you are floating on a cloud. Feeling nothing. Feeling free. Free from everything and everybody. There's nothing like it.

Whenever my Mom would freak out and scream and throw things and shit like that, all I did was go into my room and fly. She didn't even know, didn't even care. Not my Mom, no. She has other things on her mind. Too busy to notice that I was taking daily trips to LaLa land all by myself and I never had to leave the house. (*She laughs hysterically*) It's funny she would yell and scream for me to clean my room. She would come in and tear it apart and drag in buckets of bleach and make me clean it from top to bottom. I mean she did most of the work, I was too intoxicated from the bleach fumes. Yeah, bleach smells good after the first twenty minutes. Well, anyway there she was mother fucking me as she spread her joy of bleach. "You dirty sloppy bastard" she would say. "You pig" "This is how you respect my house?" "I work sixty hour weeks to keep a roof over your head and this is how you thank me?" "Why don't you thank your good for nothing Father, yeah go find the asshole and thank him for all he's done for you." "Nothing that's what he's done for you." She would go on and on as she dumped over draws and dug through my closet. (*She laughs again, even harder this time*) She did this every Saturday like clockwork at about 6 am, but not once did she ever lift up my mattress, not even when she was changing my sheets. If she had she would have been in for a sweet surprise. (*she lifts up the mattress to reveal hypodermic needles taped to the bed*) Thanks Mom, thanks to your preoccupation with bleach and a clean room your little girl still gets to fly high in her very own room in your very own house. (*Takes out a needle and prepares to shoot up*) Here's to you Mommy.

# Marie
## (14-18)

What are you scared of mom? That I won't be prom queen or the most popular girl in school? Who really cares? So what if I don't dress like I belong in a country club? What's the big deal if I get my bellybutton pierced, or if I dye my hair different colors? It doesn't make me a bad person. I'm so tired of you putting me down all the time and acting so ashamed of me. Can't you see how much that hurts? I'm your daughter. I know you wish someone else was, but unfortunately for you I am what you ended up with. Maybe things would be better between us if you started to accept who I am and get to know me. Who knows, you just might even like me. But that would scare you, right mom? Because then you would be the one who was different and your snobby friends would think there was something wrong with you because how could you possibly stand a daughter like me? Right mom? Am I right *mom*?!!! Of course, once again you have nothing to say. Well don't worry; you won't have to speak to your little disappointment forever. But one day.....  one day your gonna realize what you've missed all these years and wish you could talk to me. And fortunately for you, I will listen and allow you back into my life because I love you despite how much you disappoint me!!!

# *Ann*
## (14-18)

Look at yourself. You are a mess, a pathetic mess. And you want me to be respectful to you. You are nothing but a lousy drunk, a loser, a waste of time. You stay out all night and sleep all day. You've lost six jobs in the past three months. Two nights in a row you left the front door open and forgot to shut off the stove at least a dozen times. We could have all died not to mention the entire building. And do you even realize that our cat died last week? Yeah Fluffy died, our beloved pet, because there was no food for her. She actually starved to death and we might be next. There are no more diapers. I've been wrapping Michael in old towels and washing them at night with soap I borrowed from a neighbor. He needs you; we need you. We are hungry, tired and scared, so don't you dare ask for respect. When you start acting like a mother and take care of your family I just might give you the respect you are asking for. Until then, get out of that bed and clean yourself up and get a job. And here is a schedule of AA meetings, you have one tonight. What are you waiting for, I said get up now or I'm calling child protective services.

# *Leah*
## (14-18)

Well here I am! Ta – Da! Look at me. I'm beautiful. Don't you think? Thin, perfect, well-proportioned body. Don't you think the song I sang was beautiful and monologue stupendous? I've become quite an actor haven't I? Or...maybe I've always been one; a fabulous singer and actor. Only...you , you never saw that in me. Isn't that right Mrs Jenkens? I wasn't right for Sarah in "Guys and Dolls" or Louisa in "Sound of Music." What was it about me that wasn't quite right? Let's seeeeee.. Well....I am a much better singer than Mary Leone and a stronger actor than Susan Gold. So...what's left??? Huh! That I was FAT? Don't be shocked. You thought I was FAT, didn't you? All the parts that were ever left for me in all the school plays were the FAT GIRL, THE NERD, THE JERK everyone made fun of.

Well, (*shows off her new body*) that puts an end to your plan doesn't it Mrs Jenkins? You have no one to fill the FAT GIRLS ROLE; no one to laugh at. Sorry to ruin your plans, but look at the bright side you do have me. I'm beautiful, talented and thin. So...what's stopping you Mrs. Jenkens...CAST ME. GODDAMMIT, YOU BETTER CAST ME IN THE LEAD OR ELSE......I won't disappoint you. I'll be the perfect BELLE in "BEAUTY AND THE BEAST." Yes, I will. See you at rehearsals Mrs. Jenkens.

# *Alexandra*
## (14-18)

Please, please, please don't leave. I couldn't stand it if you left. What will I do? I might die. You can't go, not now, not ever. What did I do? Did I do something? I'm sorry if I play my music too loud or pick on Michael and Ryan, that's what big sisters do. It's in my blood. I'll stop, really I will. I'll be the best big sister you have ever seen. Is it all the time I spend on the computer? I'll stop. It's the dog isn't it or my rabbit? I'll take better care of them. Just please don't leave me. This is prime time for me. My teenage years. I may be a little off, a little strange, but it's probably just hormones; the crying and screaming and stuff, just hormones. I can be medicated or something. Just don't leave. And as for my clothes I'll wear more appropriate ones and those jeans with the holes, I'll throw them out and I'll get rid of all my slutty tee-shirts. Wholesome that's what I'll be. I'll wear GAP or Banana Republic clothes, that's wholesome and don't worry I'll get a babysitting job to pay for my new clothes and other things I want. That's it isn't? It's money. I ask for too much money. Well not anymore. Now that I'm getting a job you won't to have give me money. I'll change, I'll do whatever you want just don't go. I won't survive if you go. I don't know who to be without you. I don't know who I am without you. What will people think of me without you? They'll hate me. They'll think I'm not worth sticking around for. They'll think that if you left, you the most important person in my life, the one who is supposed to love me unconditionally walked out and didn't turn back...well, they'll think I'm nothing, somebody to avoid. See Daddy's just don't leave their girls, not their number one girls who love them and need them. Don't you remember Daddy how you used to bounce me on your knee and tell me I was your girl and that you would never leave me? Don't you remember, Daddy.

# *Rose*
## (14-18)

Different, no strange...no awkward, stupid, ridiculous, ugly or maybe...I don't know I feel it all; like an alien from outer space. I don't belong here. Every morning when I wake up I think how will I fit in, can I fit in? It feels like the rest of the world is this huge puzzle and I'm the piece that doesn't fit; the piece that was chewed up by the dog and won't ever fit no matter how hard you try to fix it or shove it in there; It just won't go, it just won't budge. Don't try to tell me all teenagers feel this way. I've heard that one a million times. "Don't worry you'll grow out of it." "I felt the exact same way when I was your age." "This too shall pass." I've heard them all and more. It doesn't help not one bit. And don't try forcing me into feeling different. Yelling at me to stop feeling this way isn't going to help either. I love that one. Who the hell yells at someone to make them feel better? (*Yells into her hands as if they are a megaphone*) "Hey you over there!" "Awkward, stupid, ridiculous teenager" "Yeah, the ugly one, over there, stop feeling like crap." "Get over it, enough already, we can't take it, you're nothing but doom and gloom and you're getting in our way." Well, go to hell. This is the way I feel and it goes way down deep into my soul and it hurts, it hurts real bad and giving me advice and yelling at me is not going to help. And you can forget about therapists, I know all about them and they're all full of crap each and every one of them. They're not me, they can't get into my skin, my insides and find something better, something worth saving. A stranger in a chair taking notes trying to figure me out. Who the hell ever thought of that? What idiot thought a total stranger who listens to you for an hour once a week could fix you all up? The concept is insane. So forget it, don't even think about it. It won't work. (*She collapses form exhaustion, but keeps going*) It just won't work, do you understand? Not now not ever.

Please don't even try. You don't have the tools to fix me you never did. I was born broken and there isn't a mechanic team in the world that can make me work. No not one. Do you hear me not one!

# *Melissa*
## (14-18)

You tell me you love me all the time and I believe you, but when you pressure me like this I am not so sure that you really do. I am only fourteen years old. I think it's just too young. I'm not ready to have sex with you, or with anyone. You're a lot older than me and I know you have needs, but my friends say that if you really loved me you would wait. So can you wait? I hope you can because I don't want to lose you. I can't lose you. You are the only source of love that I have. I don't have a father and my mom is never around. The only person who is around is you. You know that and sometimes I think you use it against me so you can get me to sleep with you.(*pause*) I'm sorry I shouldn't have said that. I don't want to hurt your feelings, really I don't! Please forgive me! It's just that I'm scared and it's hard to trust people and I (*interrupts herself*). You know what you're right. If you love me I should do this to let you know I love you too. You mean everything to me so why wouldn't I do this? Just....please, please promise to love me always because I need love. I desperately need love.

# *Danielle*
## (14-18)

I know I'm a teenager and I'm not supposed to say this but here it goes. I like school. It's fun! I love to look at how everyone is dressed and how they act and I love to know all the latest gossip and of course let's not forget about the cute boys. I love those boys. Yum, Yum! Don't look at me like that. It's all I think about! Yes, boys. Don't be so shocked. It's not like I'm doing anything or anything. I just like them. No, I take that back I love them. All different sizes and shapes of them. I don't think I ever met a boy I didn't like. I guess you can say that I am boy crazy. What's wrong with that? I mean I'm fourteen. What else is a girl supposed to do? I mean you don't want me to end up like my two best friends, do you? I mean they are wrecks. Two ships colliding into each other over and over. They hate themselves, they hate everyone else, they hate school, they hate their parents and teachers, they don't trust anybody or themselves. Yuk. Who wants to be like them? When there are boys, delicious boys, hot, hot boys. Oh, stop looking at me like that. Like you were never like that. You are so full of it. Every woman still thinks about the first boy she had a crush on. Come on, you remember that first time you held a boys hand or that first kiss. There's nothing wrong with it. It's great. Except for when you get your heart broken in two by the cutest boy in school and that hurts and it's humiliating and frustrating and it makes you want to go insane and you cry a lot and you download every sad song you can get off the computer and you just cry and cry and...that's the only bad part and then you realize in two weeks you forgot his name and then you find someone else to have a wild crush on and it starts all over. I mean come on what else is there.

# *Jessica*
## (14-18)

Did you ever get a feeling that you were destined for great things? I mean really great things. I don't mean being a doctor, lawyer, accountant or nurse. Not that those aren't great things to be. We need those kinds of people in the world, where would we be without them? These are everyday people. People, whose dreams have limits, people who don't realize that they are destined for big things. I don't think everybody feels that way or we would all be great and nobody would stand out. Me, I was meant to stand out, I was meant for great things. I can feel it. I feel it everyday, hundreds of times a day. It's not a fleeting feeling, it stays with me. I'm telling you right now I'm not your ordinary teenager. I may look like one and dress like one, but I'm not. I can't describe it, it's just there, and like right there (*she points to her heart*). Sometimes I feel like it's going to burst with excitement (*her heart*). Like I want to scream out to the rest of the world. "Look at me; I'm destined for something big, amazing, and extraordinary." "Take a look world this is the face of fame, the face of success." It feels unbelievable, but it's true, it's inside me. A day doesn't go by that I don't I feel like I could climb the world's largest mountain, swim across the world's biggest ocean. It's like I'm high on myself. Yeah, high on myself. I don't need any drugs of any kind; I've got my thoughts, my positive attitude. It's gonna happen, oh yeah. Me, bigger than life itself. It's just a matter of time. Just you wait and see. Yes, sir! Big, Bigger, Biggest. My name in lights. My face on T.V. or the big screen. Nothing too big for little old me. Look out cause I'm a comin. Like I said, I'm not your average teenager. Not ordinary in any way. (*she whispers*) Just you wait and see.

# *Tess*
## (14-18)

Hi….sorry that I've been sitting here in silence and the first thing I have been able to say is hi. I just feel this total overwhelming feeling of shock. I don't want to move. I want to stay in this spot always because I know it's the closest I am ever going to get to you again and you're hundreds of feet below me in the dirt…..where you don't deserve to be…where you shouldn't be. You should be sitting with grandma in your home. The place you've lived forever with the love of your life. Grandpa I feel cheated. Like life has played a nasty game. I've played by the rules but you have been taken from me anyway. Why did you have to be so wonderful? So kind and loving…gentle… everything that is true. I wish I could be mad at you….hate you. But I can't. If I could maybe it wouldn't hurt so much. All I do is miss you. I miss having you around for everything. I miss having someone in my life who loves me for who I am no matter what. Someone who thought everything I did was precious. I want you to tell me you love me. I need to hear you say it. I can hear your voice in my head all the time and the last thing you said to me was, "As long as grandma and I are in this world no one will ever hurt you." I believed you. I really did. But now what do I do when the world wants to hurt me? Because things in this world hurt; they do. And what is grandma gonna do? Every morning she gets up and goes about her day in the house she shared with you and you're not there. Every second she is reminded of you and….it must hurt so much. And mom. You were her daddy. What does she do without her daddy? My dad misses you too and what do me and Lauren do? What do we do? I can't stop crying and I know that's the last thing you would ever want me to do but I can't help it. I'm trying to live my life the way you did…never wasting a moment….working hard and loving my family but its hard. I want you back. I don't care that you were 93 and if one more person tells me that you were old and lived a long wonderful life so I shouldn't be sad I'm gonna scream. I don't care. I want you to live 93 more years. Because you deserve to...because the world needs people like you in it. People who really care and love their families and.... I'll stop complaining now because I know you don't like that. Can I ask you a favor though? Please watch over us. Take care of my mom and dad and sister and especially grandma. I'm scared she just wants to lie down and be with you and I know you would like that but we need her here. Please help her to be happy and enjoy the rest of her life. Well I'm gonna go. If I don't get up now I may never leave. Hopefully next time I come to visit your gravestone will be up. Oh...one more thing? Did you like the Atlantic City ticket I gave you? I hope there is an Atlantic City type place where you are. I'm sure there is in your heaven. Well before I go...I just hope....I want you to know...well. You know how you always said that what really matters is how you treat someone when they are here...because when they're gone nothing matters. Hopefully I treated you well and you knew how much I loved you. Because I love you so much and have always cherished everything about you. Heaven truly has gained a one of a kind beautiful spirit, but your family will always carry around your soul.....and death can't take that from us. I love you grandpa!

# TEEN BOYS: 14-18

# *John*
## (14-18)

Dad, just leave me alone. Go away! (*as he scrambles to hide his pot*) What do you want? Go to bed. (*his dad breaks down the door*) What the hell is wrong with you? You're drunk again. What a freakin' surprise. Get the hell out of here you bum! (*pause*) You're slurring your words so bad I have no idea what you are saying. What.... WHAT? You are gonna lecture me about my report card as you're piss drunk on the floor in my room? Just get out.....GET OUT, GET OUT!!! Leave me alone I have stuff to do. (*pause*) Why am I so angry? Because I have a piece of shit drunk for a father whose footsteps I seem to be following in because that is what everyone expects. I have had no role model; no man to look up to, a terrified mother, and all I have been taught is violence and you are gonna come in here and lecture me on my grades when I barely care enough to go to school. Screw you! Yeah you heard me SCREW YOU! You wanna hit me? Go ahead...GO AHEAD...hit me. It wouldn't be the first time and definitely won't be the last. But you better watch out. Cause one day I'm gonna hit you back and I may never be able to stop. So get the hell out of here and lecture yourself. You bug me all the time because you hope you will push me over the edge and I will fail.....fail so bad it will out shine your own failure. All of these years I thought it was me you couldn't stand but the truth is it's you that you hate. For once in my life I don't blame you because I can't stand to look at your pathetic face either. Look at me! Look at me while I'm talking to you this time. Look in my eyes.....do you hear me?!?! Yeah go ahead....throw up, pass out, break something. I don't give a shit. Just get out of my way!

# *Sheldon*
## (14-18)

So I went and got a job today at the grocery store. I'll be saving all the money and giving it to Sarah for the baby. I obviously don't pay rent at my parent's house so she can have all of it. Please tell her that when she comes home. I gotta go my brothers' waiting for me outside. (*he walks towards the door until he hears Sarah's mothers voice.*) I'm not a low life loser. I'm trying to do the right things. Right my wrongs ya know? You're always saying to me it took two to make this baby. Well why don't you tell that to yourself and your daughter. She willingly participated in everything that happened and don't tell me she didn't. I'm outta here. (*the mother says something else*) What do you want lady? You're not my mother so stop yelling at me. You know what? I think you want me to tell you some truth that's why you're pushing my buttons. You want to hear what a lousy mother you are and how Sarah followed your example and got pregnant at 16. You are a slut and now you can call your daughter one too and treat her the same way your parents treated you. Is that what you wanted to hear? Now the truth is out. How does is feel? You should know Sarah wasn't a slut. We were stupid one time but you have been repeating your mistakes. You don't think everyone sees all the men leave this house? Well you taught your daughter well and history repeats except for one thing. Unlike the guy that left you to raise Sarah on your own, I'm gonna take care of this child. So go find some other male to unleash all your pent up anger on. Go back to tricking yourself into believing your worth something and leave me alone.

# *David*
## (14-18)

Hey dad what's up? Yeah I'll talk to you in a minute…I gotta go the bathroom. One minute…..I just woke up. What's your deal? What car? What are you taking about? Let me just take a piss and I'll talk to you. Well sorry for the cursing but I just woke up and I gotta go and you're annoying me about your car. I don't know what happened to it. Why don't you ask Sean? (*pause…looking stunned*) Okay I'll sit down….chill out. Dad I'm so tired I can't even remember if I had the car last night, and so what if I did? That doesn't prove that I scratched the door. My jacket was in the car? Oh well I must have left it there yesterday afternoon. There were empty beer cans? Dad I don't even drink…I'm not even 21. I would never do that. You're not buying the "good kid too innocent to drink" thing? Just curious….what gave me away? The hang over, the fact that its 3:00 in the afternoon and I just woke up or my off the charts grades? Jesus Christ man….turn that light off. I think I'm gonna puke. Later…..leave me alone. Holy crap, turn down that music. No I don't want any eggs. I don't want anything. What is that smell? Please stop torturing me. Alright I had the car. I wasn't driving though. I have no clue who actually was, but it's home, and it's fairly safe. I'll pay for the scratches. Yes I'll get a damn job. Dad I swear I would rather buy mom tampons then go through this right now. I feel so sick. I just want to go to the bathroom and go to bed. I get it, you're doing the whole teach me a lesson so I'll get so sick I'll never drink again thing. Real cute. Not so effective but….. 'touche'. I'm going back to bed. Yes to get some rest. (*says the next line under his breath*) Yes so I'm rested to go out tonight. Umm I didn't say anything. WHAT! I'm not riding my bike. Are you crazy? No car for two months? That's bull! Yeah you're real funny. I'm not gonna 'pimp' out my bike. Please don't ever say pimp again. I get it no drinking, and taking the car and blah blah blah. Good bye. Next time I'm just gonna stay in bed and hope I don't wet it

# Jay
## (14-18)

How could I forget? It was devastating, sickening. Think about it! How could you do this to me? You did me in, tied the noose around my neck and left me for dead. I know you think this is funny but its not. I am really pissed off, really really pissed off. I could kill you. I thought you were my best friend. Is it that important to be part of a group; a crowd. They are nothing but a bunch of idiots. Yeah, I thought they were cool at first just like you. But so far they've tortured small animals, made girls cry and pranked on teachers. Poor Mr. Whitby, they blew out every one of his car tires and old lady Casey they put itching powder in her coat and gloves; almost gave her a heart attack. Yeah, they are real cool, real mature. But taking my clothes out of my locker was the last straw. It was horrible and uncalled for. Not even a towel was left for me. I mean I knew they could be capable of anything, but you? You were my best friend. Do you know I sat in that cold shower for four hours before the coach walked in. I was humiliated. I am scarred for life and as for you I don't ever want to see you again.

# *Joey*
## (14-18)

Dad, Dad, Hello it's me Joey. Remember me your son your loving devoted son? That's right, loving. Do you ever see me, I mean really see me for who I am, not just how I look or the mistakes I make. I love you Dad, all the time no matter what. When you lost your job, I was still proud of you. When you never showed up for any of my baseball games or my school plays, I never got angry or stopped loving you. I have always loved you Dad even when you hit me, kicked me, called me names or when you're so drunk you don't even know my name. Yeah, I love you Dad, do you hear me!!! I love you very much. I wish you could see through the liquor and drugs and see me, Joey your son, your child. I'm good dad. I'm smart and talented and people like me; lots of people. I only wish you did. But you couldn't, other wise you would stop drinking, take care of yourself, get help. But you don't, you won't. So, bye Dad, remember I love you. I love you daddy, that's why I am leaving. I can't watch this anymore . I can't be your punching bag, your witness to insanity, your invisible flunky. I mean I might as well shove the pills down your mouth, pour in the liquor and order a coffin. But I am done. I have to save myself, cause Lord knows I can't save you. Bye Daddy, and remember I love you.

# *Walter*
## (14-18)

There you go again. Embarrassing me. You do it so much you don't even know you're doing it. It's frightening! Today at school, did you have to come into my class with my lunch and pinch my cheeks? Then you asked for a hug in front of all my classmates. Could I look anymore like a mamma's boy? I could buy lunch you know. And speaking of lunch, nobody packs one anymore, much less gets sandwiches with the crust cut off in a brown paper bag decorated by their mommy and filled with little notes like "Have a nice day," "Be a good boy," "Mommy loves you." And the other day at football practice when I was tackled you screamed "Don't you hurt my baby, you big bully." Nothing for nothing Mom, but nobody's parents come to practices and you're there for every single one gasping at every move I make. All I hear from the stands is "Oh my God." "Ohhh, don't break his leg" "Honey, look out." And sitting out in the car waiting for me is even more embarrassing. I feel like a three year old. You have to let me grow up; no you must let me grow up. Putting my name in my underwear, shirts and socks has to stop. No more lunches, no more perfumed sachets in my gym sneakers or attaching my gloves to my coat and definitely do not make out valentines for my classmates this year. I am thirteen years old this can't go on anymore. Let your baby go. I am a man now, deal with it Mommy.

# *Doug*
## (14-18)

Oh my go…get out of here (*slams door*). Jesus mom! Why would you just open the bathroom door when you know I'm in here? (*pause*) You thought I was ready to go? If you thought that all you had to do was yell and scream for me like you normally do. STOP! Please don't say another word. This is making me sick!!! Please SHUT UP! Don't start with that 'it's a natural part of life bull. What you think you just saw, you didn't see. It really is not what it looked like and….why am I talking to you through a door? I'll be downstairs in a minute. Go away! Don't you ever give up? (*awkwardly*) If you must know I was taking the new shampoo bottle out of the cabinet and dropped it in the sink and then there were soap suds everywhere and they got all over my boxers….lots of white thick soap suds! So ummm that's what that stuff was that I was cleaning off my boxers when you came in here. You don't believe me? Well its true and that is the story that is going to be told when you tell it because I know you don't know how to keep your mouth shut. Now please….before I die of humiliation…go. I'll see you in a few minutes once my body recovers from the shock! (*pause*) For the last time ma I don't want to discuss petting the snake with you and why do you have to call it that and where the hell did you even hear that? Can't you just pretend it didn't happen like every other parent on this planet would? If you really feel the disturbingly painful need to discuss this can we do it after my football game? (*pause*) THANK YOU! Now, lets just make sure we pick up an industrial sized door lock on the way home so maybe I won't have nightmares until I'm 80.

# *Kyle*
## (14-18)

Oh, man! Is she hot. I mean red hot, on fire. OUCH! Did you see her walk down the hall this morning? Wow! Actually, come to think of it, she did not walk, she did not wiggle, she glided dude, glided. Like a sweet soft ball of ice cream gliding down a brown crunchy waffle cone, mmm, mm.

My dream woman. She is one quarter Janet Jackson, with a Mariah Carey smile, Lisa Marie Presley lips and ooh, ooh, ooh, a fine Jennifer Lopez........I am just about to make my move man. Me, I, with all my coolness all my you know macho male attitude. I mean I am ready, I am going, I am struttin' it dude. And just as I am about to make my mark. Big old half man, half woman Coach Friedman comes plopping, no stomping like some big ass elephant and grabs me and yells at the top of her ugly, smelly lungs... "Mr. Mason where were you 2$^{nd}$ period!! If you want to make it as a long distance runner, first you have to show up. Dreams don't come true if you don't put in the time." That ain't all. She grabs me by the ear and starts dragging me down the hall in front of my Janet, Mariah, Lisa, Jennifer babe. I feel like shouting Mrs. Friedman, woman you and your sewer breath have just killed my dream of kissing Miss Fine behind the bleachers after school. So with my head twisted, being dragged by fat pig woman, I watched as Mr. All That Football Captain stood by laughing with his arm around my girl. Sometimes life really sucks.

# *Chuck*
## (14-18)

(*he enters very sad*) Yeah we won the game.....7-6. I scored the game winning goal, but what the heck would you care? You weren't even there. Come to think of it you're never there...ever!(*pause... listen to father*) Of course I'm yelling. I am so sick and tired of this crap from you! I really can't deal with it anymore. I can't believe in you anymore. You're the worst father in the world! Everyone's dad came to the game. Everyones!! They've all been to just about every game. I wasn't even asking you to show up for every game. I gave up on that...on you a long time ago. But I thought maybe you would come to the most important game of my life. Maybe you would be there for once to see me shine. But you can't even do that for me. You're always so busy with work and all the other crap you do. (*Pause*) Yeah I said crap! I'm so angry I don't even care what I say to you anymore because it's obvious you don't care about me. (*pause*) Don't apologize! I don't want to hear it. Your apologies mean nothing. They're just empty words. You really disappointed me today. When the game was over I prayed that I would turn around and see your face smiling; looking so proud, but all I saw was emptiness. I hate you! I hate you so much I can't even believe that mom would marry a guy like you. Ya know what? This is over. I don't want to spend any more time on you because everyone knows you don't spend a second on me!

# *Charles*
## (14-18)

I'm not gonna chill out. You're being a complete jerk man and it's about time I said something. Yeah, I am yelling at you Jared and I'm not scared. I don't care if we are friends. It's not cool to make fun of someone who is in a wheel chair. You torture Jane everyday during gym class. How do you think she feels? (*pause*) Like crap! She obviously has been through a lot and the last thing she needs is some idiot like you bullying her. What is wrong with you anyway? How can you be so mean? (*pause*) Joking? It's not a joke and it's not funny. Remember when Cindy wouldn't go to the dance with you because you had a zit? Remember how you felt? You tried to play it off like you didn't care but I know you did. And that was just a stupid zit. By the way, do you want to know why I never invite you to my house? My sister is handi-capped and needs a wheelchair and if you even looked at her weirdly I would kill you!! So call me a loser, I don't care. But pick on me instead of Jane. Pick on someone who can fight back! Oh, and about us being boys.....forget it because I don't want to be friends with an ass like you!

# *Kenny*
## (14-18)

I am flipping out you hear me, flipping. It is my senior year and I am flipping out. Do you even know what is going on inside of me? I am learning how to drive, which scares the shit out of me because I am still afraid to walk, and college I have no idea which one to pick much less what to major in. My whole life is changing. I am going to be a grown-up soon and I am still working on figuring out the whole teenager thing. Everyone thinks I look older than I am and that I am so mature and grounded. Well, hello! I'm not grounded. I have one foot up my ass the other one spends 98% of the time in my mouth. I haven't even had a girlfriend yet and now I'm being shipped off to college. How am I supposed too survive. Challenging times you say? This is beyond challenging. Challenging is getting up before 2 p.m. on a Sunday. I can't do this and you can't make me. I have decided to stay in high school forever. I need to perfect that first before I can move on. So don't ask me what college I'm going to or what major I am picking. I don't have a clue! You are looking at one scared crazy ass teenager who is not going anywhere! It's not funny. What are you staring at me like that for? I am not kidding. I know you think you did a great job raising me and well I'll give you some credit, I will. I am a good boy, responsible, smart and well some times I appear well adjusted but you also screwed me up too. While you were busy tending to other things and your own needs I got lost in the shuffle. I feel as if I am in the middle of rush hour in Manhattan just being dragged along with the crowd. So, come on give me a hand here and do something, please! O.k., remember when I was a little boy and you used to make me hold your hand all the time so I didn't get hurt. Well, now is a good time to start holding my hand again, I can use a little help. (*he reaches out his hand*) Thank you!

# *Zachary*
## (14-18)

This sucks there is nothing to watch on television. Just a bunch of reality shows. Who wants to watch other people's reality when I got enough of my own. MTV, VHI the County Music Channel, NBC, ABC, CBS any would do. If they got a camera and followed me around the show would be called the "Life of a Lazy Ass Teenager." Well, it's what my parents call me! All I hear is: clean up your room, walk the dog, feed the dog, watch your sister, pick up your clothes, clear the table, put the dishes in the dishwasher, do your homework, iron your clothes, wash the car, mow the lawn. Well, no they don't ask me to mow the lawn our front yard alone is two acres. But if they could they would. All they do is nag, nag, nag. And it's funny, they call me lazy? I'm the one doing all the work. What am I Cinderfella?

And God forbid I go out. Be home by 10 sharp, one minute later and you are grounded for a week. All my other friends are able to stay out till midnight on the weekends and 10 on weekdays. So their a little tired the next day or can't get out of bed sometimes or maybe they're a little messed up and don't do their homework and well on occasion one gets into trouble does a little detention or gets a bad report card or ends up in jail and well some dabble in drugs. But I wouldn't do that. Not any of that. I am a responsible respectful teenager with moral and values. I would never hurt myself or anybody else and well I love my family. Why can't they let me be me and have some fun and break loose and go wild once in awhile? What you say? I am a responsible respectful teenager with morals and values. Duh! I said that already genius. Sorry that wasn't very respectful was it? (*he laughs*) What are you trying to say?

CPSIA information can be obtained at www.ICGtesting.com
Printed in the USA
LVOW101507040412

276154LV00004B/141/A